What's in your bag?

A Model's Guide and Etiquette

Preparing for a runway show is an exciting time. Getting your hair styled, manicure and pedicure or brow and body wax is the obvious, but what's in your bag?

•Let's talk about it

In a lot of cases production will have a model's hair and makeup done on set, but let's say for the sake of the argument that it's not provided. What do you bring in your bag to be sure thatp you're show ready?

In this guide we will address all necessary items and essentials that's needed for a successful runway experience.

•So, let's get right into it

We're going to start at the top and make our way down from head to toe. As I mentioned before, depending on selected or assigned styles by production you may have had your hair done prior to arrival on your own or you may be getting styled on set, but when in doubt a sleek pony style can never do no wrong. It gives designers and or makeup artists the opportunity to see your face and see exactly what they are working with. So, you will want your hair clean and neatly pulled back from your face.

You'll need hair products to achieve or refresh this look in your bag just in case you have to do your own hair. If you are wearing long tresses, you'll also need items for that look as well.

Ponytail Holders

Hair Gel

Extensions

Flat Iron

Hair Spray

Hair Pins

Comb

Brush

•Let's Face It

No one knows our faces better than us so unless you are modeling for a makeup brand that requires you to wear their specific brand, bring your own makeup. Your own foundation at least to be sure of accurate coverage and color, also in case you may have to do your own makeup. You don't have to be a pro to achieve a nice subtle runway look.

Every model should have an emergency makeup kit and the ability to achieve a soft subtle runway look. If a dramatic look is required for a particular show, it is more than likely that production will provide a MUA to achieve dramatics so no worries. In your makeup bag should be the basics.

Lip gloss (See Tips)

Blush palette	**Eyeshadow palette**
Mascara	**Eyeliner**
Lip liner	**Highlighter**
Concealer	**Foundation**
Primer	**Setting Spray**
Wipes	**Brushes**

•Shoe Game

The proper shoe is no game at all. The "shoe" even though it rarely gets the recognition it deserves in the fashion world, is the main attraction of the entire style. If the shoe 'doesn't fit, you must 'acquit' the whole look. Selecting the correct shoe is very crucial to a style. Again, as it relates to the designer and the nature of the show, it depends on whether shoes are provided.

In the case that it's not, it's better to be safe instead of sorry. Bringing your own shoes can be difficult as it comes to narrowing it down to a selected few, especially if you have many styles to choose from.

May I suggest a black heel and a nude heel to be exact, but if you or the designer may be looking for an awkwardly fashionable pop to the styles you may also like to add a color heel as well as a tall knee boot to your collection for an extra sprinkle to the style.

Black Heels

Nude Heel

Color Heels

Knee Boot Heels

•What lies beneath?

Black undergarments are not necessarily a requirement,
but it is preferred. In your bag should be a ***regular*** and
***push up bra, strapless bra, a one-piece control top
bodysuit, panties, thong, and boy cut underwear to
compliment any style selection.***

•Take Cover

It's a good idea to have a ***robe*** in your model
bag to cover up between styling changes if your
scenes are not back, to back while waiting for
your next designer or maybe not if it's a
high-volume show with rotating scenes, but
let's just put it in the bag for the sake of sitting
pretty.

•Just Throw it in the Bag

Seems like now you have everything you need, but what if you have gained or lost since your last fitting? What if you had no fitting at all? Sure, the stylist or designer should be responsible for garments properly fitting, but sometimes your garments are already hung and arranged waiting for you on racks along with other models by the dozen. You may have only minutes until showtime.

In that case you need to be fully prepared for mishaps. This is where I am supposed to suggest a mending tool case which contains a simple sewing kit, yarn or thread, a darning mushroom, and some safety pins.

But as a model in the show and not a stylist you should not be required to perform such a big task. However, you will need **safety *pins*** for quick fixes. Such as improper fittings or damaged garments.

•**Etiquette** (Good Energy)

So now that you have bagged everything, hair products, makeup, undergarments, your robe and shoe game; there's one more thing that we must touch down on and that's etiquette. A model's etiquette is having good positive energy and proper hygiene. Punctuality is your very first impression so must arrive on time.

When you show up on set you must display a level of confidence, poise, and professionalism. Listen more and talk less all while delivering a friendly disposition and good attitude towards production and the modeling team.

If you're having a bad day do everyone a favor and stay home. No one wants to be around any illicit behaviors. It affects the mood of everyone around you and sometimes carries out into the show. Production's top priority is producing a great show and bad vibes are not welcomed. Gossiping, loud talking or erratic laughter and outbursts are prohibited behaviors as well. It creates a hostile environment and makes people uncomfortable. So put your good energy in your bag too.

•**Etiquette** (*Good Hygiene*)

When it comes to hygiene it is very important and sometimes uncomfortable for adults to tell other adults what their expectations are. You are wearing garments that are up for sale, so you must be careful when wearing them. Not only to protect the garment, but also to protect yourself because another model more than likely may have worn a particular item prior to you, so pantyliners should be on your list to throw in the bag.

Next, as it applies to hygiene, try to remember to apply moisture to your skin prior to coming to set to allow time for absorption and to avoid staining garments, but still add moisturizer to your bag. Also avoid using a lot of heavy smelling perfumes and body sprays.

However, a spray on antiperspirant deodorant is advised to avoid those annoying underarm white stains we sometimes get on garments. Oftentimes, we are not aware of what the designs are for some garments, strapless dresses or sleeveless tops are bound to be on the racks so please remember to wax, shave or Nair underarm hair as well as private areas.

It is totally a necessity when preparing for a show. Be a good team player. Even if you have already paid attention to your private areas, you can still throw a few fresh razors in your bag in case another model may need to borrow. In a rush there are many things that may be left behind. Production wants everyone to look great.

When working up close and personally together there is nothing more unsettling than bad breath. Chewing gum is not acceptable, but sucking on a mint is just fine. Throw a few mints in your bag and offer one to another model as well. A mint does not necessarily mean you have bad breath, it's also a soothing and calming mechanism that can alleviate some stress. With that being said, pain killers should also be in your bag for unexpected cramps as a result of your menstrual cycle or a headache from the excitement of preparing for the show.

Pantyliners

Tampons

Moisturizer

Razors

Pain Killers

Mints

- **Etiquette** (Chin Up)

Not being selected at a model call can be very upsetting. As a model you must take it all in stride and accept it with a smile and grace. You must understand that in most cases it doesn't mean that you are not stunning or didn't qualify. It just simply means that you may not be what they are looking for at that casting.

Casting for a runway show is a lot like casting for a movie. There are specifics that production is looking for. Keep your positive energy at full blast. Do not display any hostile behavior and be mindful that the probability is that high you'll meet this team again and you would want to be considered for future projects.

•**Tips** (reference the guide)

1. *Models should wear all black to a model call.*

2. *Hair should be pulled back from the face at a model call.*

3. *Clear or Nude lip Gloss* hint: *(adding eyeshadow to clear gloss creates desired colors)*

4. *If you have an unexpected pimple, try using a black eyeliner pencil to turn it into a beauty mole.*

5. *A band aid (to cushion a shoe from rubbing the back of your foot.)*

6. ***A messy sleek back bun for a stiff weave that loss its bounce*** *(missed hair appointment)*

7. ***Stud Earrings*** *(unless otherwise is suggested by designer)*

8. ***A ponytail holder*** *(to gather a tight fit of a top around a petite model)*

9. ***Hair glue*** *(loose lashes)*

10. Clean Flat iron *(can press out unwanted creases in a garments)*

These are some potential suggestions that may be helpful to your runway experience. However, every model and designer have their own preferences and styles which makes us unique in this industry. I hope that you found *"What's in your Bag? A Model's Guide and Etiquette"* as entertaining as it was helpful as well as the added tips. Everything listed is things I have used in my own individual experiences, and I feel that they'll be beneficial to readers as well.

Good luck with your next successful venture!

NOTES....

Things to do....

Model Calls ....

www.ingramcontent.com/pod-product-compliance
Lightning Source LLC
Chambersburg PA
CBHW070025260726
48658CB00003B/1043